Written By: Anna DiGilio

All rights reserved. No part of this publication may be reproduced, distributed, or transmitted in any form or by any means, including photocopying, recording, or other electronic or mechanical methods, without the prior written permission of the publisher, except in the case of brief quotations embodied in critical reviews and certain other noncommercial uses permitted by copyright law.

For permission requests, write to the publisher:
Laprea Publishing
info@lapreapublishing.com

Website: www.GuidedReaders.com

ISBN: 978-1-64579-595-7

© 2019 Anna DiGilio

Photo Credits:
Cover, Title Page: Depositphotos; Gelpi. 3: Shutterstock; Smile Studio AP. 4 (top): Depositphotos; Pressmaster. 4 (bottom): Depositphotos; CITAlliance. 5: Shutterstock; G-Stock Studio. 6 (top): Depositphotos; Szefei. 6 (bottom): Depositphotos; AntonioGuillemF. 7 (top): Shutterstock; Fizkes. 7 (bottom): Depositphotos; Lisafx. 8 (top): Depositphotos; Alekseykh. 8 (bottom): Shutterstock; AJP. 9: Depositphotos; McAndy. 10 (top): Depositphotos; Serrnovik. 10 (bottom): Shutterstock; Ruslana Iurchenko. 11: Depositphotos; Karelnoppe. 12 (top): Shutterstock; Stock photo by Yaa. 12 (bottom): Depositphotos; Ivash. 13 (top): Depositphotos; Georgemuresan. 13 (bottom): Shutterstock; Rawpixel.com.

TABLE OF CONTENTS

What Can a Face Say?.................Page 6

Glossary..Page 14

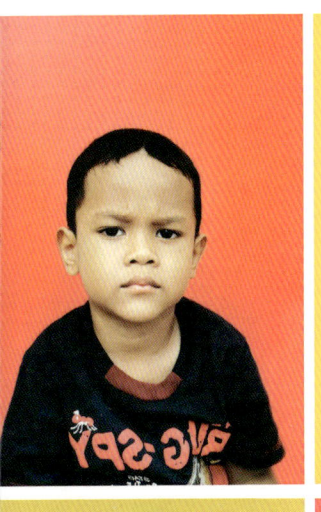

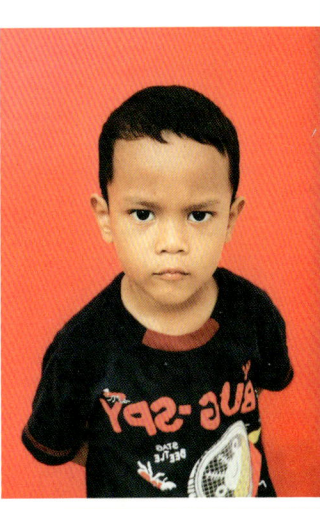
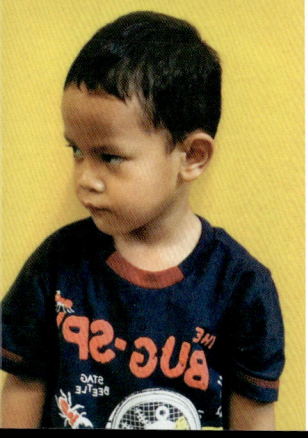

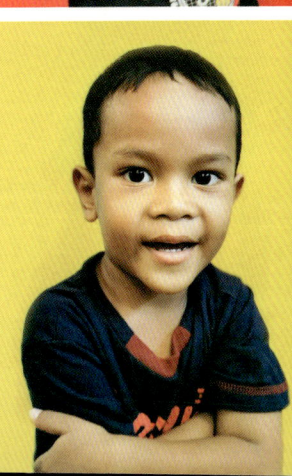

You can read books. You can read maps.

You can read faces. Faces give you <u>clues</u>.

What Can a Face Say?
Faces tell how someone's feeling.

Upset

See the <u>frown</u>? Someone is <u>upset</u>. They may be angry.

Angry

7

See the eyebrows? They are up. They are surprised.

The eyebrows are down. That's a clue. It means someone is angry.

See the big smile? Someone is happy.

Uh-oh. Wet eyes. The lips are <u>smushed</u>. Someone is crying.

Breaking a toy can make a child cry.

You can cry for many reasons. You may be sad. You may be mad. You may be joyful!

A bride may cry because she is happy!

Look at faces. They tell you a lot. They are a map to <u>feelings</u>!

GLOSSARY

<u>clues</u>
pieces of evidence that leads one toward the solution of a problem

<u>feelings</u>
emotional states or reactions

<u>frown</u>
an expression of unhappiness

<u>smushed</u>
mashed or pushed

<u>upset</u>
a state of being unhappy, disappointed, or worried